THE 2012 LONDON
OLYMPICS

Nick Hunter

Heinemann
LIBRARY

Chicago, Illinois

www.heinemannraintree.com
Visit our website to find out more information about Heinemann-Raintree books.

To order:
☎ Phone 888-454-2279
💻 Visit www.heinemannraintree.com to browse our catalog and order online.

Edited by Kate de Villiers and Laura Knowles
Designed by Richard Parker
Picture research by Liz Alexander
Production by Camilla Crask
Originated by Capstone Global Library Ltd
Printed and bound in China by CTPS

15 14 13 12 11
10 9 8 7 6 5 4 3 2

Library of Congress Cataloging-in-Publication Data
Hunter, Nick.
  The 2012 London Olympics / Nick Hunter.
    p. cm.—(The Olympics)
  Includes bibliographical references and index.
  ISBN 978-1-4109-4119-0 (hc)—ISBN 978-1-4109-4125-1 (pb)
  1. Olympic Games (30th: 2012 : London, England)—Juvenile literature. I. Title.
  GV7222012 .H86 2012
  796.48—dc22   2010049491

Acknowledgments
We would like to thank the following for permission to reproduce photographs: Alamy p. **19** (© Jim West); Corbis pp. **9** (© Stephen Hird/Reuters), **11** (© Elizabeth Kreutz/NewSport), **13** (© Sampics), **16** (© London 2012/Handout/Reuters), **18** (© Erich Schlegel/Dallas Morning News), **24** (© Chen Xiaowei/Xinhua Press), **27** (© HO/Reuters); Getty Images pp. **12** (Jamie McDonald), **14** (David Goddard), **15** (Mark Dadswell), **17** (Adrian Dennis/AFP), **21** (Al Bello), **23** (Feng Li), **25** (Feng Li), **26** (Julian Finney), Mary Evans Picture Library pp. **7** (Francis Frith); Press Association Images p. **4** (AP Photo/ Max Nash); Shutterstock p. **5** (© r.nagy).

Cover photograph of the Aquatics Center for the London 2012 Olympics reproduced with permission of Getty Images/London 2012.

Every effort has been made to contact copyright holders of material reproduced in this book. Any omissions will be rectified in subsequent printings if notice is given to the publisher.

Disclaimer
All the Internet addresses (URLs) given in this book were valid at the time of going to press. However, due to the dynamic nature of the Internet, some addresses may have changed, or sites may have changed or ceased to exist since publication. While the author and publisher regret any inconvenience this may cause readers, no responsibility for any such changes can be accepted by either the author or the publisher.

Contents

Some words are shown in bold, **like this**. You can find them in the glossary on page 30.

Countdown to 2012

The tension was incredible. After many years, the decision was about to be made. Which city would host the Olympic Games in 2012? Most people expected Paris to win. The **bid** team waited nervously as the announcement came:

*"The **International Olympic Committee** has the honor of announcing that the Games of the Thirtieth **Olympiad** are awarded to the city of ... London."*

No one in the United Kingdom could believe it. The world's greatest sporting event would be coming to London! Thousands of athletes from more than 200 countries would meet in London to prove who was best in their chosen sport.

A huge crowd in London's Trafalgar Square celebrated wildly as the announcement was made that London would host the Olympics in 2012.

Hosting the Olympics

There was little time for celebration. There was a lot of work to do before London could welcome the world in 2012. The **Olympic Park** had to be built in east London, including a **stadium** and swimming center. The organizing team had to plan every last detail, from the timetable of sports to the **security** needed for such a massive event.

Why London won

The London Olympics team wanted to use sports to inspire young people. The bid team included then Prime Minister Tony Blair, sports stars, such as David Beckham, and children from east London.

London's Olympic History

London is the first city to be chosen to host the Olympic Games three times.

London 1908

The Olympics were in crisis when the Games first came to London in 1908. The 1904 Games in St. Louis, Missouri, had been a disaster. London's preparations started late when Rome, Italy, dropped out of holding the Games.

The biggest controversy came in the **marathon**, when spectators carried the exhausted leader, Dorando Pietri, across the line. The popular Pietri was **disqualified**. The marathon was actually extended by 385 yards (352 meters) so it finished in front of the Royal Box. Since then, 26 miles and 385 yards (42.2 kilometers) has been the standard distance for the marathon.

Post-war Games

When the Games came to London in 1948, the city and much of Europe was being rebuilt after World War II. Money was tight and athletes stayed in army camps and schools. This was very different from the new **Olympic Village** planned for the London 2012 Games.

Much Wenlock

Before the modern Olympic Games began in 1896, the Much Wenlock Olympian Games were held in the small town of Much Wenlock (above) in Shropshire, United Kingdom, from 1850. This sporting festival was an important inspiration for Pierre de Coubertin, who started the modern Olympics.

Bidding for the Olympics

The **International Olympic Committee (IOC)** makes the decision about who will host the Games. **Bid** teams have to convince most members of the IOC that their city is the best place for the Games. A small team began to prepare London's bid in 2003.

Winning the Olympics

The cities that wanted to host the 2012 Olympic Games made their presentation to the IOC in Singapore. Lord Sebastian Coe, the leader of the bid, said the London Olympics would inspire young people to take up sports. The team had a nervous wait to see if they had won the bid. Once the announcement was made, the real work began, to make the bid a reality.

SEBASTIAN COE
(BORN 1956)

Before leading the London Olympic bid, Sebastian Coe was already one of Great Britain's greatest athletes. He won Olympic gold medals in the 1,500 meters in 1980 and 1984. After retiring from athletics, Coe was successful in politics and sports administration. He was the perfect choice to win the bid for the Games.

Thirty children from London took part in the Olympic bid. Because London's people come from so many countries, they "represent the youth of the world."

From Beijing to London

At the closing ceremony of the 2008 Olympic Games in Beijing, China, the mayor of Beijing handed the Olympic flag to Boris Johnson, the mayor of London. The five rings on the flag represent the joining together of all countries in the **Olympic Movement**. The world's athletes were invited to meet in London in 2012.

Thousands of people were already working on building the **Olympic Park** and other sporting venues. The **Olympic Village**, the media center, and transportation links to and from the Olympics also had to be built.

A global event

All aspects of the Games have to be planned to make sure that 300 events go smoothly in front of a massive television audience around the world. Every organizing committee wants their city to look its best. A huge **security** operation is also planned to protect athletes and spectators.

The Olympic torch relay

The Olympic flame is lit using the Sun's rays at Olympia, Greece. Then 8,000 athletes carry it to London, each taking the burning **torch** for a short part of its journey. The final athlete will carry a lit torch into the **stadium** at the opening ceremony on July 27, 2012. Then he or she will light the Olympic flame that will stay lit throughout the Games.

Boris Johnson, the mayor of London, accepts the Olympic flag at the closing ceremony of the Beijing Olympic Games in 2008.

Olympic Sports

When many people think of the Olympic Games, they think of athletics. Around 2,000 athletes are expected to compete for 47 gold medals in the running, jumping, and throwing events at the London Olympics.

Doing a Rudolph

There is much more to the Olympics than the 100 meters or the long jump. The London 2012 Games will feature 26 sports and around 300 individual events. Just 32 athletes are expected to compete in the trampolining competition. They will perform amazing somersaults and flips with names such as Adolph and Rudolph.

The 2012 Olympic archery competition will be held at Lord's Cricket Ground.

Animal athletes

Many events require special equipment, but the **equestrian** events and modern **pentathlon** are the only ones that involve animals. More than 200 horses will compete in these events at the London Olympics. Athletes in the modern pentathlon have to compete in fencing, swimming, running, and shooting, as well as horse riding.

Handball is a fast-paced team sport. It is popular across Europe.

Changing sports

The list of Olympic sports can change. Baseball and softball will not be part of the London Games after the IOC voted to remove them. Other ex-Olympic sports include cricket, in which Great Britain beat France in the only Olympic competition in 1900, and **tug-of-war**, which featured between 1900 and 1920.

Olympic Venues

The London 2012 Olympic Games and **Paralympic** Games will be held at many different venues across London and around the United Kingdom. Many of these are being specially built for the Games.

Olympic Park

The **Olympic Park** has been built on land that was once used by industry. It is now home to nine new Olympic venues, including the Olympic **Stadium**, the Aquatics Center for swimming and diving, and the Velodrome for track cycling. The stadium will hold 80,000 spectators for the opening and closing ceremonies and the athletics events.

The Aquatics Center will save water by using waste water from the pools to flush the toilets.

The park also includes the **Olympic Village**, where many of the 10,000 athletes will live during the Games. The whole area has been designed to be kind to the environment, with its own energy center and green spaces to provide **habitats** for plants and animals.

GOING FOR GOLD: JESSICA ENNIS

Nationality: British
Date of birth: January 28, 1986
Event: **Heptathlon**

Jessica Ennis is the World and European champion in the heptathlon. She will have to compete in seven different athletic events in just two days: 100-meter hurdles, high jump, shot put, 200-meter sprint, long jump, javelin, and 800-meter run. London will be Jessica's first Olympics, as she missed the Beijing Games because of an injury.

Across the city

There are also many Olympic venues across London, including some historic landmarks. Greenwich Park will host the **equestrian** events. Horse Guards Parade ground, close to Buckingham Palace, will be transformed into an arena for beach volleyball.

Other athletes will compete in famous sporting venues. The tennis competition will take place at Wimbledon, home of the famous tennis tournament. Wembley **Stadium** will stage the finals of the Olympic soccer competitions. The sailing events will be held on the south coast of the United Kingdom at Weymouth and Portland.

Horse Guards Parade is the home of the soldiers who guard the Queen. In 2012, around 15,000 people will come here to watch the beach volleyball event.

Welcoming visitors

The United Kingdom expects to see more than 320,000 extra overseas visitors at these venues during the Olympics. There is even official advice on welcoming visitors. The advice warns Britons not to take offense at Argentinian humor, and that people from Belgium may consider it rude if you snap your fingers.

GOING FOR GOLD: RAFAEL NADAL

Nationality: Spanish
Date of birth: June 3, 1986
Event: Tennis

Rafael Nadal has won almost every competition in tennis, including a gold medal at the Beijing Olympics in 2008. He has also won the Wimbledon tournament. Despite his many titles, Nadal will still only be 26 in 2012. He will be looking to retain his Olympic title.

The Athletes

London will welcome more than 10,000 athletes from around the world. Some will be expecting to win gold medals; others will be happy just to take part. Teams such as China, the United States, Canada, and Australia will send hundreds of athletes. Other teams will be much smaller. Dominica's team at Beijing in 2008 had only two athletes.

At the opening ceremony, athletes parade behind the flags of their countries. At the closing ceremony, they mix together to enter the **stadium**.

The Olympic dream

Winning an Olympic medal takes years of training. Athletes train every day just to be good enough to compete at the Olympics. Swimmers and runners often train for hours before a full day of work or school. They must eat the right things and avoid injuries, hoping to be in peak condition when the Games begin in London.

Training, training, and more training! This U.S. boxer trains for the Olympics at a special center in Michigan.

Life in the Olympic Village

During the Games, 17,000 athletes and officials will live in the **Olympic Village**. The village includes green spaces, restaurants, and training areas. For many athletes, mixing together in the village is one of the best parts of the Games. Some, such as the tennis legend Roger Federer, have even met their future wife or husband in the Olympic Village.

Old and new

Many of the 2012 athletes will be competing at their first Olympics. Medalists in events such as gymnastics and swimming are often teenagers. The youngest swimmer at the Beijing Olympics was just 12 years old.

There will be others trying to repeat performances at previous Olympics. British Olympians, such as Scotland's cycling legend, Chris Hoy, are especially excited. London 2012 will give them their only opportunity to win gold in front of a home crowd. Hoy already has four gold medals, but hopes to win again in London.

Olympic spirit

Many medal-winners benefit from government funding and high-tech training techniques. Other athletes can only dream of these luxuries. Swimmer Eric Moussambani of Equatorial Guinea competed in the 100-meter freestyle at Sydney in 2000. He had to train in a 20-meter hotel pool, which he could only use when the hotel guests were not there. He had never raced more than 50 meters. Eric's time was more than a minute slower than the faster swimmers, but his joy in taking part showed true Olympic spirit.

I want to be an Olympic champion!

Many athletes dream about being an Olympic champion from a very early age. To turn that dream into reality, every Olympic athlete puts in many hours of training and has to eat a healthy diet. Those who stand on the medal podium have to combine talent for their sport with a fierce will to win.

GOING FOR GOLD: USAIN BOLT

Nationality: Jamaican
Date of birth: August 21, 1986
Event: 100 and 200 meters

Usain ("Lightning") Bolt was the biggest star of the Beijing Olympics. He won the 100 and 200 meters in world record times, and charmed the crowd. He also won relay gold. Can he repeat this amazing performance in 2012?

The Paralympics

London in 2012 will host not one but *two* great festivals of sport. On August 29, shortly after the close of the Olympic Games, the Olympic **Stadium** will be the scene of the opening ceremony of the **Paralympic Games**. The Paralympics bring together the best athletes with disabilities from around the world. Competition is just as fierce as at the Olympic Games.

The biggest ever

The London Paralympics are expected to be the biggest ever. More than 4,000 athletes will compete in the Olympic venues and stay in the **Olympic Village**. All Olympic venues and the village need to be accessible to wheelchair users and other Paralympians. The build-up to the Games will include a **torch** relay around the United Kingdom.

Paralympic history

In 2012 London will host the first official Paralympics in the United Kingdom. The country has a special place in the development of Paralympic sports. In 1948, as the Olympic Games started in London, a contest for World War II **veterans** who had suffered **spinal injuries** took place in Stoke Mandeville, Buckinghamshire. This was the birth of Paralympic sports. The first full Paralympics were held in Rome in 1960. The Paralympics have used the same site as the Olympic Games since 1988.

Paralympic athletes are extremely fit and determined sportspeople, who just happen to have a disability. Here, **visually impaired** soccer players are playing a five-a-side match.

Paralympic values

Like the **Olympic Movement**, the Paralympic Games acts as a great inspiration to young people. The Paralympic Movement tries to break down social barriers around disability. Anyone who watches the Paralympics will be inspired by the determination and skill of Paralympians in overcoming their disabilities.

Paralympic sports

There are 20 different sports scheduled for the London **Paralympic Games**. Most sports are divided into different classifications, depending on the disabilities of the athletes, for example wheelchair athletes and **visually impaired** athletes. Some, such as wheelchair basketball or five-a-side soccer for the visually impaired, are only open to one classification of athletes. The largest number of athletes competes in the athletics competition, which includes wheelchair races from 100 meters up to the **marathon**.

Because of the different classifications, there are more medal events at the Paralympics than at the Olympic Games. In 2008 in Beijing, 473 gold medals were awarded. British athletes finished second in the medal table, behind China. The U.S. team finished third.

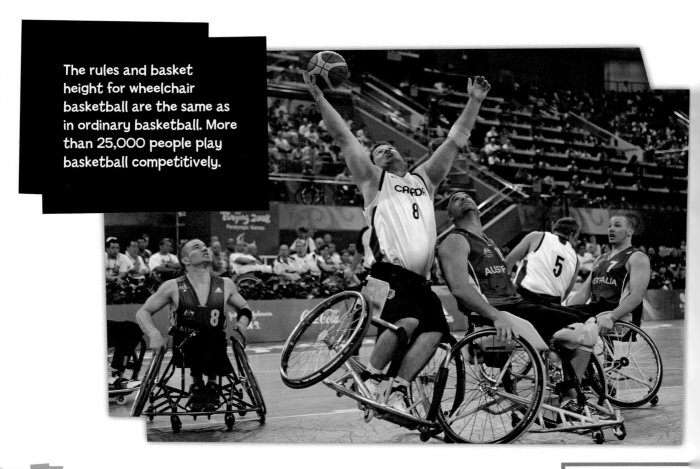

The rules and basket height for wheelchair basketball are the same as in ordinary basketball. More than 25,000 people play basketball competitively.

GOING FOR GOLD: ELEANOR SIMMONDS

Nationality: British
Date of birth: November 11, 1994
Event: Paralympic swimming
Eleanor Simmonds will be just 17 years old at the Paralympics in 2012. At the age of 13, she became Britain's youngest ever Olympic or Paralympic champion. She won gold in the 100-meter and 400-meter freestyle (S6 category) at the 2008 Paralympics. Since Beijing, Eleanor has been named the BBC's Young Sports Personality of the Year (2008) and awarded an **MBE** by the Queen.

The Legacy

When the London Olympics have finished, what will happen next? The organizers hope the Games will leave great sports arenas for Londoners and the United Kingdom. The **Olympic Park** will remain as a green space for the people of London.

Olympic heroes

They also hope young people across the world will find new heroes in the athletes competing in London. We can't all be Olympic champions, but the Olympics may persuade people to take up sports and change their lives for the better. As Sebastian Coe said in 2005, "To make an Olympic champion takes millions of young people around the world to be inspired to choose Olympic sport."

Olympic mascots

London has two Olympic mascots. Wenlock (left) is named after Much Wenlock, the home of the forerunner to the modern Olympic Games (see page 7). Mandeville (right) is named after Stoke Mandeville, where the first unofficial Paralympics took place in 1948.

The **Olympic Movement** hopes that the amazing performances in this London stadium in 2012 will inspire young people to take up sports.

Where next?

At the closing ceremony of the London Olympics on August 12, 2012, the Olympic flag will be passed to Rio de Janeiro in Brazil. Rio will become the first South American city to host the Summer Olympics in 2016. Sochi in Russia will hold the Winter Olympics in 2014.

London–Olympic City

Venues and sports

Olympic Park

- Olympic **Stadium** (athletics)
- Aquatics Center (diving, swimming, synchronized swimming)
- Velodrome (track cycling)
- There are also venues in the **Olympic Park** for basketball, BMX racing, handball, hockey, and water polo

Around London

- Earl's Court (volleyball)
- ExCeL Exhibition Center (boxing, fencing, judo, table tennis, tae kwon do, weightlifting, wrestling)
- Greenwich Park (**equestrian** events)
- Horse Guards Parade (beach volleyball)
- Hyde Park (**triathlon**, 10-kilometer **marathon** swimming)
- Lord's Cricket Ground (archery)
- North Greenwich Arena (gymnastics, trampolining)
- Royal Artillery Barracks (shooting)
- Wembley Arena (badminton, rhythmic gymnastics)
- Wembley Stadium (soccer)
- Wimbledon (tennis)

Around the United Kingdom

- Eton Dorney, Berkshire (rowing, canoe sprint)
- Hadleigh Farm, Essex (mountain biking)
- Lee Valley White Water Center, Hertfordshire (canoe slalom)
- Weymouth and Portland (sailing)
- Various stadiums including Millenium Stadium, Cardiff and Hampden Park, Glasgow (soccer)

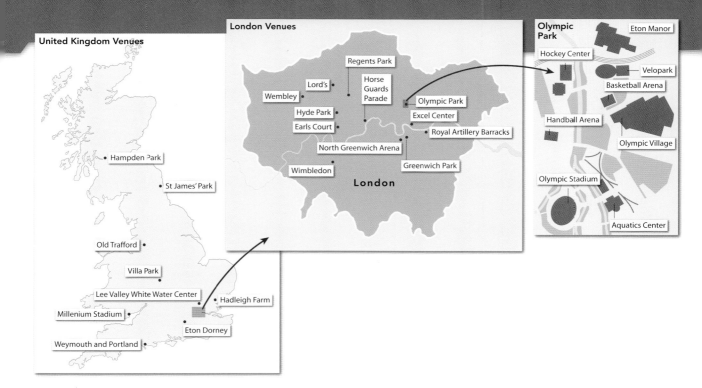

Countdown to the London Olympics, 2012

776 BCE	The first Olympic Games are held in Olympia, ancient Greece. The Games are held for more than 1,000 years before they are abolished in 393 CE.
1896	The first modern Olympic Games take place in Athens, Greece.
1908	London hosts the Olympic Games for the first time.
1948	London hosts the Olympic Games for the second time. A competition for disabled athletes is held at Stoke Mandeville, Buckinghamshire. This would later become the **Paralympic Games**.
1960	The first Paralympics are held in Rome.
July 6, 2005	The **IOC** announces that the Olympic Games will be held in London in 2012.
August 24, 2008	At the closing ceremony of the Beijing Olympics, the Olympic flag is handed over to the mayor of London as the next host of the Olympic Games.
July 27, 2012	Opening ceremony of the London Olympic Games.

Glossary

bid attempt or campaign, in this case the campaign to bring the Olympics to London

disqualify stop someone from being part of a race or competition because they have broken the rules

equestrian on horseback or relating to horses

habitat place where an animal or plant lives

heptathlon contest for women athletes that has seven events

International Olympic Committee (IOC) organization that runs the Olympic Games and decides where they will be held

marathon long running race held over 26 miles and 385 yards (42.2 kilometers)

MBE stands for Member of the Order of the British Empire. This is an honor given by the British monarch to people who have achieved something remarkable.

Olympiad period of four years leading up to the Olympic Games

Olympic Movement all the people involved in the Olympic Games, including the International Olympic Committee, Olympic officials from each country, and each Olympic sport

Olympic Park area in London where many of the Olympic venues are built, including the Olympic Stadium and the Aquatics Center

Olympic Village specially built housing where athletes and officials live during the Olympic Games

Paralympic Games games for athletes with a disability, held after the Olympic Games in the same place

pentathlon sports contest with five events, usually swimming, cross-country riding, running, fencing, and pistol shooting

security keeping people safe

spinal injury injury to the spinal cord in the back or neck that can cause people to be paralyzed and need to use a wheelchair

stadium large arena for sporting events. The Olympic Stadium is used for athletic events and the opening and closing ceremonies.

torch something held in the hand with a light or flame at one end

triathlon sports contest with three events, usually swimming, running, and cycling

tug-of-war contest between two teams pulling on either end of a rope. The winner is the team that pulls hardest on the rope.

veteran person who has fought in a war

visually impaired disability affecting the sight, such as total loss of sight

Find Out More

Books

Christopher, Matt. *The Olympics: Legendary Sports Events*. New York: Little, Brown Books for Young Readers, 2008.

Gifford, Clive. *Summer Olympics: The Definitive Guide to the World's Greatest Sports Celebration*. New York: Kingfisher, 2004.

Macy, Sue. *Freeze Frame: A Photographic History of the Winter Olympics*. Washington, D.C.: National Geographic Children's Books, 2006.

Macy, Sue. *Swifter, Higher, Stronger: A Photographic History of the Summer Olympics*. Washington, D.C.: National Geographic Children's Books, 2008.

Websites

www.london2012.com
The website of the London Olympics includes details of venues and preparations for the London Games, as well as information about Olympic sports.

www.olympic.org
The official website of the International Olympic Committee includes facts and statistics about every Olympic Games and every medal winner.

news.bbc.co.uk/cbbcnews/hi/sport
This BBC site includes sports news for young people. It will keep you up-to-date with the Olympics.

To find out about the different sports that will be a part of the 2012 Olympics, you can search for the organizations that govern each sport. For example, you can find out more about athletics at: **www.iaaf.org**.

Index